joinedupwriting

ROGER MCGOUGH

PENGUIN BOOKS

PENGUIN BOOKS

UK | USA | Canada | Ireland | Australia
India | New Zealand | South Africa

Penguin Books is part of the Penguin Random House group of companies
whose addresses can be found at global.penguinrandomhouse.com.

First published Viking 2019
Published in Penguin Books 2019
001

Copyright © Roger McGough, 2019

The moral right of the author has been asserted

Printed and bound in Great Britain by Clays Ltd, Elcograf S.p.A.

A CIP catalogue record for this book is available from the British Library

ISBN: 978–0–241–37421–4

www.greenpenguin.co.uk

Penguin Random House is committed to a
sustainable future for our business, our readers
and our planet. This book is made from Forest
Stewardship Council® certified paper.

joinedupwriting

From the first tentative scratch on the wall
To the final hurried, unfinished scrawl:
One poem.

Defying Gravity, 1992

Contents

The Ginsberg Skeleton

After 'The Ballad of the Skeletons' by Allen Ginsberg

Said the FIFA skeleton
Hide the whistle and line our pockets
Said the Arms-dealer skeleton
Sell them mortars, tanks and rockets

Said the Dope-dealer skeleton
I can't cope with the demand
Said the False Prophet skeleton
It is written in the sand

Said the Tobacco skeleton
There's a billion lungs to fill
Said the ISIS skeleton
That's what we do, we kill

Said the Whip-cracking skeleton
Love that lip-smacking blood
Said the Beheading skeleton
It's just like chopping wood

Said the Far Right skeleton
We must keep them at the borders
Said the Tear Gas skeleton
I'm just obeying orders

I

Said the People-smuggler skeleton
I put freedom within reach
Said the Washed-up skeleton
They found me on the beach

Said the Ebola skeleton
Sorry, I'm not finished yet
Said the World Bank skeleton
You can breathe when you've paid your debt

Said the NRA skeleton
It's a basic human right
Said the Bullet-riddled skeleton
Yup, damn right

Said the Schoolgirl skeleton
I wish we'd never met
Said the Grooming skeleton
What you see ain't what you get

Said the Self-harming skeleton
The blade cuts out the ache in me
Said the Jesus skeleton
Why hast thou forsaken me?

Said the Payday skeleton
Keep on taking out the loans
Said the skeleton of colour
Am I the token bones?

Said the Harley Street skeleton
You could never afford my fee
Said the Lying-in-state skeleton
What you see is what you'll be

Said the skeleton in the cupboard
Who locked me up in here?
Said the Brexit skeleton
It seemed a good idea

Said the Plagiarised skeleton
I'll call the poetry police
Said the Ginsberg skeleton
Now let me rest in peace

Said the Ginsberg skeleton
Now let me rest in peace.

I Hear America Sighing

After 'I Hear America Singing' by Walt Whitman

I hear America sighing, the varied complaints I hear.
Those of mechanics, each one bemoaning his as he walks away
from the shut-down factory. The carpenter bewailing his
as he boards up another broken shop window. The matron
in the hospital barking hers, harking back to the days of Obama.
The boatmen lamenting theirs, nets full of plastic bags and bottles.
The celebrity tweeting hers about the intrusion of privacy.
The banker howling his like the ghost of a wolf on Wall Street.
The shoemaker grumbling his as his son buys another pair
of Adidas trainers. The bellyaching of the blame-throwers.
The keening chorus of mothers grieving for murdered sons.
Each crying what belongs to him or her and to no one else.

America, I grew up with you, you my brash elder brother,
Superhero, singing in the rain from the Halls of Montezuma
to the shores of Tripoli, from the sands of Iwo Jima to
a Coney Island of the mind. Star-spangled romantic,
laconic wisecracker, go-getter, no sooner said than done.
Now the wisdom, has it cracked? The getting, has it gone?
The stars have dimmed, no moon ahead. Oh, say!
Can you dance by the light of the rocket's red glare?
Flags furled, insults hurled, banners waved in anger.
In Times Square the wind moans, and all around the sound
of groaning, the earth trembling as the screen fades to black.
Stop sighing, America, start singing. Time to come back.

That Poem You were Writing

It's not easy being a poet nowadays.
Especially if you wander away from the desk
and pick up a newspaper, or listen to the radio,
switch on the TV, or be drawn into conversation.

That poem you were writing,
the one about your father taking you to the Stadium
as a kid to watch the boxing, and his annoyance
because you wanted to leave before the final bout.

(Jimmy Doyle a welterweight whose father
worked with yours on the docks.) Like Jimmy,
the poem was promising, as you negotiated the line
between memory and nostalgia, honesty and regret.

If not ringside seats, close enough to feel
the smack of leather, the gobs of sweat.
To feel cold jabs of nausea and the need to escape.
Without a word to your father, you wander away from the desk.

That poem you were writing,
still there on your return, but unrecognisable.
In the ring, Trump slugs it out with Kim Jong-un.
In the Ladies, Weinstein exposes himself to a suicide bomber.

To put an end to the nonsense, you climb into the ring
only for Jimmy Doyle to fell you with a single blow to the chin.

Confusion

Am I the only one who's confused?

(Pause)

A thigh bone the size of Cleopatra's Needle
unearthed in Patagonia. Novichok in Salisbury.
Scones and polonium tea in Mayfair.
In Duluth, a tattooist tattoos his initials
on the whites of his girlfriend's eyes.

(Pause)

Another boat filled with migrants capsizes.
Shares soar, there's a plummeting pound
(the morning after, the other way round).
If you're not British, best get packing.
Build more runways, let's get fracking.

(Pause)

'HUNDREDS LOST ON CRUISE SHIP IN MEDITERRANEAN'
screams newspaper headline. Turns out there was
only one winner on the SS *Saga Rose* that night
when Mrs Beryl Crossley from Leeds won six bingo
games in succession. 'I were reet chuffed,' she said.

(Pause)

A swan in Suffolk swallows a hot coal.
In Duluth, partially sighted girl
seeks new boyfriend with initials M.W.
Have I been transgender all these years
and nobody had the decency to tell me?
Am I the only one who's confused?

(Pause)

Obviously not.

Three Cheers for the Cheerleaders

Who cheers up the cheerleaders
when their team has lost the game?
When the star wide-receiver
has suddenly gone lame?

Who cheers up the cheerleaders
when the cheerful mask slips?
Wipes the tears of the running back
When he stumbles and trips?

Who cheers up the cheerleaders
when the home fans hiss and boo?
Makes the tight ends giggle
when they're feeling sad and blue?

Who cheers up the cheerleaders
when they're down in the dumps?
Gently rubs liniment
into the quarterback's lumps?

Who cheers up the cheerleaders' leader
after nine games lost in a row?
(Probably one of the linebackers,
to be honest I really don't know.)

But I do know how much we shall miss them
when they put their pom poms away,
So three hearty cheers for the cheerleaders
Hip hip . . . Hip hip . . .

The Full English

Perhaps I shouldn't have been drinking Guinness and eating olives
when I did the swab test for my DNA. The results confirmed
what I had long suspected, a dearth of Englishness.

69.6% Irish and Scottish? No surprises there, I suppose.
A *Mc* in the name is a sporran stuffed with shamrock.
But 12.5% Spanish, Italian and Greek?

A Roman soldier, centurion I imagine, sweeping my great, great
great, etc. granma off her feet after a ceilidh in Connemara,
with promises of sea, sand and sunshine? Hardly.

Quickie on a peat bog in the pouring rain, more like.
Only 17.9% English? I can't believe it, that's only half a buttockful.
What polite hostility kept my forebears at a distance?

Immigrants over here under sufferance.
Mass-goers with a propensity for large families
and drink. Accents that goaded the neighbours.

But let me be thankful for this heady genetic cocktail.
A pinch of Plato, a sliver of Virgil, a little Lorca
and a cement-mixer full of cheek and blarney.

Unable to face the Full English, I push the fry-up aside
And, taking out Grandad's little tin whistle put it to my lips.
Failing, as ever, to get a decent tune out of it.

The Overall Winner

I remember wondering, aged eighteen months,
as the Lady Mayoress crowned me
'Overall Winner of the Bootle & District Bonny Baby Show'
if life would be downhill from then on.

My mother, posing proudly for the *Echo* photographer,
would seldom feel so fulfilled.
One arm around her prize-winning son,
the other holding the prize, a pair of khaki overalls.

No crawling races, rattle-throwing or dummy-catching,
no tricky questions, no need to impress or outfox.
All I had been required to do was smile
and not fill my pants.

By and large, life skills that have stood me
in good stead over the years.
But on a daily basis I miss the unsolicited adulation,
the warm consolation of my mother's arm.

The overalls? I never did find a use for them.

PS Fake Poetry

Hold on there. Overalls?
The first prize was a pair of overalls?

It's called poetic licence.
The prize was actually an electric iron.

Big deal. It's a wonder your mother
didn't hit the Lady Mayoress over the head with it.

You must remember, there was a war on
and household appliances were rare.

First on your street to own one, I suppose?
Your father must have been delighted.

Trouble was, we didn't have electricity,
So Mum used to heat it up on the gas hob.

Fake poetry.

Of Protestants

You knew where you were at Holy Cross Junior School.
The world was divided into Catholics, by far the best,
and those doomed to a life of bewilderment, emptiness
and eventual damnation, the rest.

Jews were fine, but only Catholic ones
like the Twelve Apostles and the Virgin Mary.
Muslims mysterious, Buddhists weird,
but of Protestants, one had to be wary.

King Herod, for example, Judas and Henry 8th,
Rangers fans, the average bobby on the beat,
serial killers, and those big, rough boys
from the tech. at the end of our street.

Then the whisper that Hitler had been a Catholic.
Robespierre, Guy Fawkes, Mussolini, Al Capone?
My faith suddenly being put to the test.
So one morning in class I asked Sister Malone.

Smack! 'Protestants, the lot of them.' Smack!
'Burning in hell as sure as night follows day.'
Then softly, 'Not to worry, I won't tell your parents.
Now stand up everybody and let us pray . . .

'In the name of the Father, and of the Son, and of the Holy Ghost . . .

A Dish Best Served Cold

After the war, many men went straight from active service
into teaching. A leap too far in some cases.
At our school the demobbed fell into two categories,
the humourless disciplinarians, and the mildly demented.

'Old Joe' Kelly taught General Science to the lower school
and if he had tales to tell about his time in Burma
he kept them to himself. A loner, it was rumoured
he'd ended up in a Japanese prisoner-of-war camp.

Lunchtimes he would spend in the pub,
before returning to eat his sandwiches at his desk.
Head down, he would crouch behind the upturned lid
and mumble scientific jumbo with his mouth full.

The brightest boy in our class was called Lo.
Norman Lo, half-Liverpool, half-Chinese.
Reading quietly, good as gold, he was ill-prepared
for the aerial attack about to take place that day.

It was a bitingly cold afternoon in December,
When Joe, drink taken, lurched into the room,
and stumbling between the rows of desks,
smacked Norman hard on the back of the head.

'What's that for, sir?' cried Lo.
'Pearl Harbor,' said Joe.

Brasso

While my sister was polishing the lino
or outside in the yard chopping wood,
I would settle down in the back kitchen
with the *Echo* spread out on the table
and begin my weekly chore.

Some rags, a tin of Brasso, and before me
the family hoard: two candlesticks, ashtray,
coal scuttle, toasting fork and small handbell
from Llangollen in the shape of a lady
wearing the national costume of Wales.

My favourite I saved until last,
a German clock encased in solid brass
that had seen action during the war.
Requisitioned by dockers from a U-boat
handcuffed to the Pier Head. How I polished it.

The rub of the rag, the thrum of the engine,
the ticking of the clock. My courage
was about to be tested. The commander
downed periscope and gutturalled:
'Oberleutnant, vot time ist?'

'According to this heavy rectangular clock
badly in need of a polish, it is fünf past drei.'
'Time then for action. Achtung! Fire!
Das Boot shuddered as its torpedoes
Streaked towards a convoy of our brave lads.

'Tauchen! Tauchen!' came the order as depth charges
exploded all around. The windows rattled
and the crockery shook on the kitchen shelf.
In the yard outside a dog howled.
I dived beneath the table and held my breath.

On the count of zehn we resurfaced,
and while the crew went on deck to surrender
I stayed below and wrapped the clock in dirty rags
before smuggling it into the front room
where it shines in pride of place to this very day.

Queen Elizabeth I Visits Merseyside in 1949

Where are they now, the good citizens of Crosby
who greeted me with such warmth and favour?
The cockle wenches who sprinkled rose petals before my feet?
The soldiers of the Royal Guard?

Where are they now, my faithful courtiers?
Lord Gloucester, fat as a globe, who stumbled
when bowing low, sending his cap spinning
across the lawn like a blue velvet frisbee.

Where the roll of parchment upon which
I had written my speech? Lop-sided throne,
newly painted and sticky to the touch?
Whither the groundlings, my faithful retainers?

Whither the voice unbroken, the cheeks unshaved?
Where is Miss Allen, who tried in vain
to teach me how to act like a monarch?
'Head up, Roger, speak slowly and clearly.'

And amdrams later, after all those schoolboys
dressed as girls, the real thing in my arms.
The stage set and a full moon. 'Head up, Roger.'
Another lead role, another lead balloon.

The Bridle Path at Litherland

Bunking off school for the afternoon
We'd take our bikes for a ride
Scorching along the bridle path
The murky canal at our side.

Courting couples caught in action
Tramps and narrowboats we spied
We saw fish and birds and gypsy boys,
But never once, a bride.

Mermaid and Chips

We had half a dozen chippies
within walking distance of home.
The nearest was the dearest.
A penny more on the fish, stingy with the chips,
and no mushy peas, we gave *The Friary* a wide berth.

Mr Clarke, who limped and chain-smoked
in the *Happy Plaice*, was as sour as his pickled eggs.
Known as 'Spit-in-the-boiler', his dark shop
we avoided like the plague. (Although,
in defence of the grumpy emphysema sufferer,
it was said that the infected phlegm
would have been rendered harmless by the boiling fat.)

The *Lobster Shell* with its takeaway paper napkins
and finicky wooden forks? Too pretentious.
And the *Chip Suey*, where Mai Lai lost her dentures
shouting at a pan of curry sauce? Too risky.

Our chosen chippy, *Turner's*, was a family affair,
with Ted a showman, at home on the range.
In front of which he entertained the queue
behind him with a stream of quips
delivered into the steamed-up mirror.
'Flippin' chips,' he would say, doing just that.

The temperature of the smoking fat he gauged
with a callused finger, before committing to the deep
the batter-shrouded cod. A master of the guillotine,
he sliced spuds for scallops, while his wife
and young Linda in overalls, salt-bright and spotless,
divvied out the crisp, golden hoard.

Despite my school uniform, Linda took a shine to me.
Extra chips were a matter of course, not to mention
the odd fishcake. But I wanted more than scraps.
As mum and daughter worked behind a counter
we only saw them from the waist up
and I dreamed of Linda as a mermaid,
half-woman, half-haddock. Big breasts
and a silvery fishtail in place of down there.

Quiet Kittens

Behind NHS frames, a pink plastic eyepatch.
Deaf, she wore a hearing aid, switched on
only when the priest came to visit.

Hands, gnarled by arthritis, were turkey claws
with which she lifted a huge teapot, sawed bread
and dealt cards from the bottom of the pack.

When she lost her toes, the hospital prescribed
surgical boots. Heavy, black leather lace-ups
she wouldn't be seen dead in.

Instead, a visit to Freeman, Hardy & Willis
with Uncle George, to bring home a pair
of Quiet Kittens several sizes too big.

'You mean Hush Puppies, Gran?' we shouted.
Resourceful to the end, she stuffed the gaps
with cotton wool and shuffled on for years.

Aunt Bridie Goes to Heaven

And let us not forget Aunt Bridie,
who is still with us, thanks be to God.
Eighty-nine and still going strong.
Wrong. Weak, but eighty-nine and still going.
And knowing exactly where she's going. To heaven.

You don't spend great chunks of your life
hunched in prayer, or on your knees in church,
without gaining a sense of direction.
You don't mix with the cream of Irish clergy
without gaining some insight into life everlasting.

Having outlived seven siblings, two husbands
and an only child, she is no stranger to the deathbed.
Each night she rehearses that final scene
and worries about falling into a coma and missing it.
Worries too about the new priest, a good and holy man
by all accounts, but West African.

And when the Angel finally calls, Aunt Bridie will slip away.
And if St Peter's not there waiting, there'll be bloody hell to pay.

Come January

Come January I'm not at my best.
The time of the year I'm put to the test.
Body swaddled in layers of clothing,
self-coddled I waddle, filled with self-loathing.

I look to the sky, it should be ash grey,
but it's shamelessly blue, as if to say:
'I'm just the backdrop, la mise en scène
for long summer days that will soon come again.'

Come Spring, comes the welcoming first sunny spell.
'Cold comfort,' I mutter, curling up in my shell.

Closing In

A bleak midwinter in mid-March
The broken promise of Spring's warm embrace

Black ice and the roads closed to traffic
Thick fog and a sky free of planes

The consoling silence interrupted
by a wind with a gale-force chip on its shoulder

Birds in the know have flown, the sticklers
tight-beaked, fastened to bare branches

For fear of being outnumbered
children have stopped building snowmen

Above the Thames, a drone, frozen in mid-flight,
drops like a stone, smacks through the ice

On the lawn, a snow leopard
lies in wait for the fox cubs

Who is that on the horizon
staggering through the blizzard?

Can it be April? April to the rescue?
Sadly, no. A snowman closing in on a lost child.

PS Pathetic

Hold on there. A snow leopard
in a suburban garden in west London?

So the poem says.

And does the poem say how it got there?

No.

Have you informed the authorities?

No, my main concern was to rescue the child
from the clutches of the evil snowman.

And did you?

No.

Pathetic.

The Perfect Negative

In search of the perfect slug
I left no stone unturned

In search of the perfect butter
I left no milk unchurned

In search of the perfect firefighter
I left no house unburned

In search of the perfect match
I left no lover unspurned

In search of the perfect fool
I left no face ungurned

In search of the perfect ending
I left no lesson unlearned

In search of the perfect negative
I left No.

My Little Bird

After 'My Little Wife' by Anon.

I had a little wife,
    The prettiest ever seen
She washed up all the dishes,
    And kept the house clean.
She went to the mill
    To fetch me some flour,
And always got home
    In less than an hour.
She baked me my bread,
    She brewed me my ale,
She sat by the fire
    And told many a fine tale.

*

Then one day without a word
    She flew away, my little bird.
Now who will do my cooking?
    Who will brew my ale?
Who will bring a happy ending
    To this sorry tale?

'Not I,' cried the widow
    'Nor me,' cried the maid
'Nor us,' cried the ladies
    Marching on parade.

The Villain of the Piece

Who seduced then deserted my favourite niece?
The two-timing villain of the piece

Who doubled the rent then cancelled the lease?
The landlord villain of the piece

Who broke into a house and stole the Matisse?
The discerning villain of the piece

Who shopped his best friend to the local police?
The two-faced villain of the piece

Who force-fed foie gras to the neighbour's geese?
The gourmet villain of the piece

Who vowed to go straight after his release?
The wayward villain of the piece

Who shaved his head and became obese?
The hideaway villain of the piece

Who robbed a bank then fled to Greece?
The feckless villain of the piece

Who met and remarried my clueless niece?
The millionaire villain of the piece.

One Rainy Morning in April

Don't ask me how he managed
to corkscrew his way
through the pavement
on Kensington High Street,
but there he was:

Stranded, this huge fish.
His fin, three-cornered,
A piece of sheet-iron.
Row upon row of
Knife-edged teeth.

At first, thrashing, slamming
the once crowded sidewalk.
Now circling, uncoiling.
Pedestrians run for safety.
One, not quite quick enough.

One Hot Afternoon in Late August

How he slipped unnoticed through
the ticket barrier at Hammersmith
one can only guess, but there he was
on the Piccadilly Line train to Cockfosters.

Passengers huddled together at one end
of the carriage, leaving him enough space
to stretch and doze fitfully at the other.
Occasionally, he would growl and flick his tail.

Why nobody called the police or alerted
the train crew remains a mystery,
but we sighed with relief and tried not to stare
when the lion alighted at Leicester Square.

One Unseasonably Sunny Day in March

Boat-race day, and supporters
line up on the banks of the Thames
from Putney Pier to Chiswick Bridge.

What the race officials hadn't expected,
nor television crews anticipated,
was the sudden and terrifying sight

of twenty or so crocodiles surfacing
beneath Barnes Bridge and swimming
downriver towards the oncoming boats.

Both crews, their backs to the danger
and misinterpreting the horror-stricken faces
of the coxes, increased the stroke-rate.

'*Crocogators!*' portmanteaued the crowd.
Too late. The first met the leading boat
(light blue, as it happens) head on.

It rose like a praying mantis, before overturning.
The plucky would-have-been runners-up
met the same fate three strokes later.

A giant saltwater captured on Eel Pie Island
some days after the carnage could offer
no assistance regarding the police enquiry.

One Mild Morning in Early November

How a troop suddenly appeared out of nowhere
in the heart of East Hackney beggars belief.
But in less than a minute Broadway Market
was engulfed in a tsunami of silverbacks.

Stalls overturned and tables swept aside.
Organic vegetables slapped and torn apart
as the mob knuckle-strutted down the street.

Hipsters and baristas ran for cover
as teeth bared and shrieking with delight,
the young swung from awning to awning,
scattering lattes and gluten-free cakes.

As sirens blared and armed men came running
the gorillas disappeared into the mist
that hung like a reprimand across London Fields.

Levelling the Cleat

I

Dear Virginia,

A good friend of ours in her mid-fifties has become involved
with a man whom we consider most unsuitable. Whereas she is highly
intelligent and privately educated, he is a jobbing roofer,
who prior to moving in with her was apparently homeless.

It is not the disparity of class that concerns us however,
but rather, his character, which is volatile and unstable to say the least.
Is he an alcoholic we ask ourselves? Has he a history of addiction?
Worse still, is he prone to violence?

We hesitate to raise the matter with Julia, a widow who has been lonely
for some years, and who seems unaware of his glaring character faults.
Perhaps of course, she is well aware, but chooses to ignore them
for the sake of companionship. Is that the mystery of love? Is it?

She alone in the house, re-reading a Thomas Hardy, he on the roof
checking the verge overhang, the flashings and the underlay.
Stripped to the waist and tanned, shingle tar on shoulders,
screeding and packing, levelling the cleat.

Replacing the battens and butt-joints, the flashings and aprons.
Darkening sky, storm clouds gather. With a fistful of nails he strives
to keep his balance in the harsh wind that threatens to topple
and dash him to the ground like a fractured chimney stack.

Is that what love is Virginia? Is it? Is it? Say that it is.
Advise them not to interfere.

Tell them to mind their own business and let love run its course.

Yours,

A well-wisher

II

Dear Well-wisher,

Thank you for your interesting letter which arrived at a most fortuitous moment. Early yesterday morning I noticed a small damp patch on the ceiling of one of the upstairs bedrooms, and deducing from your postcode that we live in the same area, I would be obliged if you could pop over at your earliest convenience and examine my butt-joints, not to mention my verge overhang, which may be in need of some TLC.

Best wishes,

Virginia

Mindfulness

Mindful of my newfound mindfulness
I awoke to the infinite possibilities shimmering
in the exquisite web of interconnectedness.

As soon as my feet touched the floor
I knew it was going to be a good day.
'Today will be a good day,' I intoned.

I went to the window, not for fresh air
but for light. I filled my lungs with pure light
and intoned: 'Today will be a good day.'

And again: 'Today will be a great day.'
And it might have been, had the Governor
not turned down my application for parole.

The Importance of Timing

On the road

Step off the pavement and stand between a line of parked cars.
Wait until you hear the one with your name on approaching.
Timing is essential. Too soon and it will either stop
or swerve past, too late and you will walk into the side.
Get it right and you will be mown down. Bang. All over.

On the Underground

Stand near the edge of the platform nearest to the tunnel
from which the train will emerge. The clue is in the noise.
As it increases move further forward and before the wind
pushes you away, either topple like a broken chimney
or dive open-armed as if into a welcoming pool.

On the railway line

You might consider leaping from a bridge into the path
of an oncoming train, but the chances are you will land
on top of a carriage and bounce off. Embarrassing.
Better to wait beside the track until it is in full view,
then step boldly between the rails to face it head on.

In all cases avoid looking at the driver: he or she
does not deserve to inherit your nightmares.

Ringing the Changes

Shocking wasn't it, to hear about the man
who committed suicide on Saturday night
by jumping off the church tower?

No coincidence it seemed, that the sight
of a body, bloodied and broken, would horrify
church-goers first thing Sunday morning.

Except for the fact that he was a bell-ringer
who lived alone and suffered from bouts
of severe depression, little is known of him.

In the interests of the couple getting married
in church the following Wednesday,
the news was brushed under the flagstones.

The service went ahead as planned
and wedding photographs taken on the steps
outside gave no hint as to the tragedy.

At the request of the vicar and out of respect
for the deceased, there was no confetti,
and church bells remained silent.

But in an act of ecumenical solidarity
those of the Catholic church down the road
rang out in muted celebration.

The following day the flagstones were replaced
and the news released, by which time
the newly-weds were winging their way to Sicily.

The Point

The point is,
the point of the story,
the point of the story is the snake.
If he had turned the car around when he saw it
and driven straight back home, it might never have happened.
But he didn't. And it did. Which is the point.

The reason,
the reason they were there,
the reason they were there in the first place
is because France is where they met and fell in love.
Had they not met it would never have happened.
But they did. And it did. Which is the point.

London,
back in London he taught French,
while she began a career as a professional cellist.
Years later, on a whim, they bought a holiday home in Provence.
Had they chosen Devon this might never have happened.
But they didn't. And it did. Which is the point.

Multiple sclerosis,
ambushed by sclerosis
insidious and incurable, it ended her career.
He gave up teaching and they moved permanently to France.
Had they stayed in London it certainly wouldn't have happened.
Not like this. But they didn't. So it did.

Quarrel,
the morning in question,
the morning in question began with a quarrel.
She remained in her room, he set the table for breakfast.
She remained in her room, he drove to the village for croissants.
Had they not fallen out, who knows? But they did, which is the point.

The snake,
the snake on the road,
stretched out on the road. An ill omen.
Aware of local superstition, he slowed down,
beeped his horn, then put his foot on the accelerator.
Had he stopped. Who knows? It might never have happened.

The journey,
the journey back,
the journey back was uneventful.
There was no sign of the snake, no blood trail, no roadkill.
He parked the car, called her name and entered the cottage.
The smell of coffee, the scent of lavender. The sound of running water.

The bath,
the bath was filled with water,
filled with water and flowers.
And in it floated her body. Ophelia-like in white nightdress.
Next to the bath her wheelchair. He pulled her out.
Pulled out the body that slid to the floor. Turned off the tap.

The point,
the point of the story,
the point of the story is a poem.
Not this poem, which is a sketchy narrative
of events that may or may not have taken place,
but the poem he read out that November morning.

Creative writing?
Fact or fiction?
The rest of the group wanted to know.
Murder? Suicide? The snake, real or imagined?
They needed the truth. 'That's the point,'
he said. 'That's what I'm here to find out.'

Late Night Nightmare

Glad to be away from it all, some years slip by unnoticed,
while others fidget awkwardly in the memory.
1968 and, as echoes of the Mersey Sound reach London,
I receive an unexpected invitation from the BBC
to appear on *Late Night Line-Up*. I am flattered.

This rather highbrow but popular television programme
went out live every Sunday night and featured
a number of guests discussing the arts and various topics.

I did worry of course, during lunch on the train
down from Lime Street (packet of crisps and four cans of lager),
if I would be able to hold my own among the metropolitan elite,
or was I the token Northerner, the Scouse poet
whose pretensions were to be exposed in front of millions?

And here I am in the Green Room at TV Centre
with 'the thinking man's crumpet' Joan Bakewell,
who tries in vain to put me at my ease as she introduces . . .

'Sir Edward Boyle and Yehudi Menuhin'.
Unsure of whether to bow or curtsey,
I half-genuflect and realise with a sinking feeling
that I have more in common with the custard
creams on the table than with my fellow guests.

'Wine? No thanks, do you have any lager?'
Need a wee, but best hang on until the last minute,
because you won't be able to go once the show starts.

Five minutes before we go on air, I head for the Gents.
I'm just installed, unzipped and, as they say in ceramic circles,
pointing percy at the porcelain, when Yehudi rushes in
and stands next to me. Suddenly I get writer's block,
as he chats away and micturates melodiously.

Still talking, he puts the finely tuned instrument
back into its case and goes to the washbasin.
I let out a pretend sigh of relief and follow him to the studio.

At the time I hadn't seen Tom Stoppard's *Rosencrantz
and Guildenstern*, nor Alan Bennett's *Forty Years On*,
nor had I read Norman Mailer's *Armies of the Night*,
or *Cancer Ward* by Solzhenitsyn, and so had nothing
to add to the lively discussion that followed.

I have always been an attentive listener
as opposed to a fearless talker, an asset appreciated
at a hospital bedside, but less so on live chat shows.

I listened and nodded wisely, I smiled and tutted
as conversation ranged from Vivaldi to Vietnam,
from Tai Chi to Tchaikovsky. Seated between them
I was like a spectator at Wimbledon, as the pair
lobbed, volleyed, smashed and served verbal aces.

Not only did my neck ache, but I was finding it
increasingly difficult to concentrate on anything
save the half-gallon of lager fermenting in my bladder.

When would they start talking about Everton, I wondered,
or at least ask me what the Aintree Iron was?
Suddenly it was my turn to walk out on to Centre Court.
Had I been inspired to write a poem about the recent
assassination of Robert Kennedy? asked Joan.

'Er . . . no, but I do have one called "At Lunchtime"
about people making love on a bus when they thought
the world was coming to an end.'

But time was against us, she was afraid. Thanked the guests
and bid the viewers goodnight. Before the credits had finished rolling,
I was out of the studio, down the corridor and into the Gents.
And guess who was up there on the rostrum before me,
baton in hand, conducting Handel's *Water Music*?   Yes.

The Bee, the Wasp and the Poet

Buzz at window
Trapped bee
Poet rises
Sets it free

Wasp at window
Can't get through it
Exit poet
Leaves it to it.

★ ★ ★

Wasp army
Lies in wait
Tired poet
Returning late

What happens next?
Bet you know it
End of poem
End of poet.

Poem to be Stitched inside a French Beret

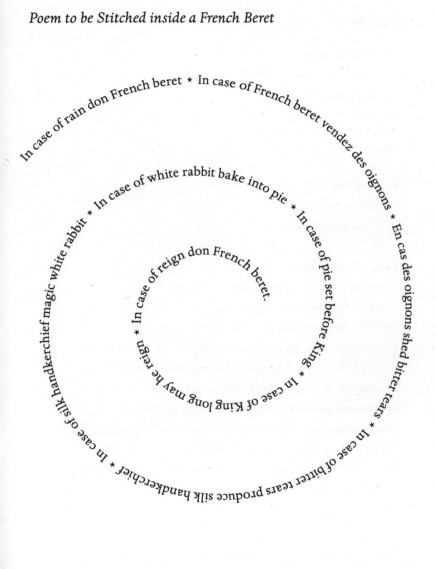

In case of rain don French beret ★ In case of French beret vendez des oignons ★ En cas des oignons shed bitter tears ★ In case of bitter tears produce silk handkerchief ★ In case of silk handkerchief magic white rabbit ★ In case of white rabbit bake into pie ★ In case of pie set before King ★ In case of King long may he reign ★ In case of reign don French beret.

One Breath

(To be read out loud)

If
If I'd
If I'd known
If I'd known the
If I'd known the poem
If I'd known the poem was
If I'd known the poem was going
If I'd known the poem was going to
If I'd known the poem was going to last
If I'd known the poem was going to last as
If I'd known the poem was going to last as long
If I'd known the poem was going to last as long as
If I'd known the poem was going to last as long as this
If I'd known the poem was going to last as long as this I'd
If I'd known the poem was going to last as long as this I'd have
If I'd known the poem was going to last as long as this I'd have taken
If I'd known the poem was going to last as long as this I'd have taken a
If I'd known the poem was going to last as long as this I'd have taken a deeper
If I'd known the poem was going to last as long as this I'd have taken a deeper breath.

Firing Blanks

If you have no interest in literature, poetry in particular,
the chances are that you will never read this poem.
Perhaps you scarcely read at all? Or are unable to?
You don't speak the language? Perhaps you are dead,
having passed away some years before publication?
Not even born yet? Now there's a thought.

And when you are, and you grow up to be a fine person,
there will be more to occupy you than skimming through
a book of old poems. If you never read this poem
what will you have missed? The intimacy that exists,
allegedly, between reader and writer? The chance
to impress friends with a few lines learned by heart?

For a poem written but unread, let us give thanks,
and spare a thought for the poet, innocently firing blanks.

What Keeps Me Awake at Night

What keeps me awake at night
are not questions like (yes, you guessed)
What keeps you awake at night? but
What will your last poem be about?

I get out of bed, open the curtains,
and try to outstare the moon.
As you are writing it, will you know
it is going to be your last poem?

Invariably I blink first. But not always.
And if you did, would you spend more time on it?
Should the moon blink first, usually towards dawn,
it's game over and back to bed.

Do you think that poems have to rhyme?

Word Bank Incorporated

Mounting anger and disbelief greeted the news last night
That Word Bank Incorporated now own the copyright on language.

Language we thought like the air we breathe, was in the public domain and free,
But since the patent has been registered, its use involves a fee.

Words, whether written or spoken, be it English or Japanese,
The Company now own them and can charge whatever they please.

A 5p rate will be imposed on the ones most commonly used,
Like *Hello*, *Yes* and *No*, though grunting and nodding are excused.

10p on obscurest words favoured by poets and dons
Like *tendril*, *brillig*, *synaesthetic*, and it's a pound on those four-letter ones.

A language licence must be purchased if you're intending to speak,
Available at the Post Office from the beginning of next week.

Wardens wearing plain clothes will patrol each city street
And using word-detectors catch those who attempt to cheat.

Anyone guilty of infringement, whether innocent or not,
Will be issued with a talking ticket, and fined right there on the spot.

Word Bank Incorporated, the dreaded WBI
I determined to confront its Chairman and ask him *Why? Why? Why?*

He was counting out his money. He stopped, looked up at me,
Glanced at his word-detector, then smiled: 'That will be 15p.'

The Facetious Carbuncle

'What is your favourite and least favourite word?'

Facetious with all five vowels in the right order
is a clever word and it knows it.
Used sneeringly with a final 'shush'
it brooks no argument.

Carbuncle, on the other hand,
can't make up its mind what it means.
Boil? Gemstone? Mythical dragon?
Nothing to do with cars, carbs or uncles.

Finding themselves in the title of a poem,
both words are confused, especially carbuncle
which for good reason, feels exposed.
Facetious, however, saunters into the spotlight,

Removes its vowels and shamelessly **F C T S**.

This is One of Those Poems

in which the title is, in fact, the opening line
and what appears to be the first line is really the second.
Failing to spot this literary device may cause the reader,

unnerved and confused, to give up halfway through
and turn to another poem with a titillating title.
Or, and this is more likely, throw the book across
the room vowing never to read poetry again.

The power of titles should never be underestimated.
'The Charge of the Light Brigade' is a good one.
'The Wreck of the Deutschland' is another.
'La Belle Dame sans Merci', however, is just showing off.

'Ode on a Grecian Urn' fails on many counts,
I mean, who's interested? Kipling's 'If—'? Iffy.
As for Shakespeare and his sonnets, *33? 84? 116?*
Well, that's just downright laziness.

The Power of Poetry

The initial aim of my appointment as Poet-in-Residence for British Telecom in 2000 was to encourage staff to write poems and email them to me, a sort of creative online workshop. Unfortunately, my appointment coincided with the sacking of a large number of employees as part of a major restructuring of the company.

Dear Harry,

Thank you for the poem.
Deeply felt, the sense of outrage and anger is palpable.
I wonder, though, if the passion occasionally overrides
and obfuscates the argument you wish to make?
And it must be said that the use of the F-word fourteen times
in a sonnet serves to unbalance the otherwise lyrical
qualities to be found therein. Worth some revision, perhaps?

*PS In the neat envoi that rounds off the poem, I think
you will agree that the C-word does not rhyme with CEO.*

Dear Linda,

Thank you for the seventeen haikus I received this morning.
I warmed to the playfulness of the idea, seventeen haikus each
containing seventeen syllables as the form dictates. Wonderful!
However, your choice of the word *sh*t* for each syllable,
although adding to the rhythm and musicality of the form,
is limiting, and 289 *sh*ts* strays too far from the essence
of haiku as exemplified by Bashō (seventeenth century).

Dear Kimberly,

First of all, a few words about the poem that came to you
'as in a dream, and which I dashed off in a single sitting'.
The title, although memorable, sent out the warning signals:
'Making Horlicks for Martin Amis'. I think you will discover
(and sorry to be the bearer of bad news) that Wendy Cope
published an identical poem in her 1986 collection entitled
'Making Cocoa for Kingsley Amis'. I am sure plagiarism
was not your intention, so moving on . . .

Yours was a lovely letter and thank you for the offer,
but at the moment I am not seeking an assistant,
or *live-in muse* as you put it. Perhaps you were misled
by the rakish poet who features in some of my early verses?
I must confess that the philandering, would-be Byron
has moved on in years and is now in a stable relationship.
However, the photographs of yourself attached,
(WHOARR! as the *Sun* would have it), I will keep on file,
should my domestic arrangements change in the near future.

Dear Luke,

I am sorry to learn that you are now out of work,
or 'thrown on to the crap heap', as you put it
in the impassioned email that accompanied your limerick
entitled 'There was a Fat Tw*t from BT'.
And again, sorry, but in my role as online Poet-in-Residence,
I am not in a position to plead on your behalf for reinstatement.
Yes, as you rightly point out, I have frequently extolled
the power of poetry, but I fear on this occasion
your recent employers may have reached for the off switch.

How Shall I Compare Thee?

Shall I compare thee to a summer storm?
The sudden squall that spoils the village fete?
The downpour drenching bride and groom,
bouquets sodden, canapés limp and wet?

The long-awaited cricket match. The barbecue,
the picnic that's been planned for ages.
You arrive uninvited, and on cue
lightning cleaves the sky and thunder rages.

Why the need to disassemble and cause trouble?
Why does the happiness of others cause vexation?
To ridicule, pour water, burst the bubble
at any friendly gathering or celebration.

What shall I compare thee to? Shakespeare knows:
Hellebore. It's in the name, a poisonous winter rose.

What Poverty My Muse Brings Forth

A cento for W.S.

O, from what power hast thou this powerful might
O, how thy worth with manners may I sing
O, how I faint when I of you do write
Farewell, thou art too dear for my possessing.
If thou survive my well-contented day
Who is it that says most, which can say more?
How heavy do I journey on the way
Like as the waves make towards the pebbled shore.
Those lines that I before have writ do lie
Weary with toil, I haste me to my bed.
Tired with all of these, for restful death I cry
No longer mourn for me when I am dead.
Poor soul, the centre of my sinful earth
Alack, what poverty my Muse brings forth.

PS RoboPoet

Correct me if I'm wrong, but haven't you merely rearranged
fourteen lines lifted from Shakespeare's sonnets?

That's what a cento is. From the Latin word for 'patchwork'.

A robot could be programmed to do that.

Not as easy as it looks. Note the strict rhyming scheme
and clear narrative.

Narrative? What narrative?

Hooking together those famous opening lines
to create a lucid reflection on writer's block.

If you say so. Milton next is it? Keats? Tennyson?
*Switch on Poet. Press **Cento**.*

Not to Mention Brexit

How a fully grown python got into the boot
of the Peugeot we will never know.
It certainly wasn't there when I loaded the cases
on leaving the hotel in Sidmouth.

One short stop for selfies at Stonehenge
plus a comfort break at a service station on the M3
and four hours later, unloading the car in the driveway,
it is wrapping itself around Rosemary's leg.

I helped her hobble into the house, where,
uncoiled, it chased the cat down the hall
through the cat flap and out into the garden.
As we speak, Rosemary lies in a heap on the patio.

I try ringing the emergency services, the RSPCA,
the Wildlife Trust and David Attenborough, but in vain.
They have their hands full with snow leopards,
lions, sharks, crocodiles and gorillas.

Not to mention Brexit.
What is the world coming to? I ask.

For Charles Causley on His Seventieth

There's a statue of Mary Magdalene
Outside a church in Launceston
And whenever the poet goes walking by
The saint sits up, and with a grin lets fly

a pebble. An ancient custom in reverse.
A playful tease to please the man
Who many love but few can match.
A word juggler who never misses a catch.

Making magic and music wherever he goes,
He sits at the foot of England and tickles its toes.

Feamus

The honesty. The cloak of fame he bore effortlessly.
The sense of calm he brought to saloon and palace.
The erudition and the sanctified craic of language.
St Francis, he could mend the broken wings of words.

Perhaps inevitably, he inspired not only love but envy.
Fellow poets admired him and acknowledged their debt.
A giant in our midst no one could deny.
And yet, and yet . . .

The thought occurred, stifled at first and then whispered
around pub tables where English poets gathered,
that had they been gifted a field of potatoes
in which to dig, a South Derry accent and a tractor,

grown up with the smell of dung, urine and buttermilk
in their nostrils, as a boy ridden horse and cart
to Ballyscullion, Moneyneany and Killaloo,
then who knows what each of them might have achieved?

They toasted the sad passing of a great poet,
finished their Guinness and took tubes and buses
back to Kilburn, Mile End and Homerton.

Lunch with the Laureate

'New collection published today,' he said,
and picking up a knife and fork,
tore into the imaginary book
on the empty plate before him.

'And you can bet some young critic,
eager to make a name for himself
is sitting down right now and sharpening
his claws before tearing it to pieces.'

'But you're Ted Hughes,' I thought.
The Ted Hughes. Who would have the gall
to attack a new collection of poems by you?'

'But you're Ted Hughes,' I said.
'Does it really matter what some jealous
metropolitan, would-be poet thinks or says?'

The main course arrives.
Fox cutlets, stuffed crow, wolf brains.
Unnerving, but delicious.

Aubade Mirabilis

Needler Hall, the University of Hull

Woken at dawn to the sound of Bechet's clarinet
coming from his room on the floor above,
as the door opens and he creeps down the stairs.

The flop of moth-eaten brocade slippers
along the corridor. The knock. The 'Come in'.
He stands in the doorway, plain as a wardrobe.

'Thought you might be able to help.'
He stays just on the edge of vision,
an unfocussed blur, a standing chill.

There is no escape. The curtain-edges grow light
and the room takes shape. 'Work has to be done.
What year was the Beatle's first LP?'

'Nineteen sixty-three,' I mumble.
'*ABBAB*. Excellent.' And he is gone.
The sky is white as clay, with no sun.

Charlie and the Chaplain

For a brief period during the end of the nineteenth century, while his parents were playing the music halls in Liverpool, the young Charlie Chaplin attended school at St Francis Xavier's Church. Fr Gerard Manley Hopkins was there around the same time as priest and school chaplain.

Chaplain! Chaplain!
Yes, Chaplin?
Chaplain! Chaplain!
What is it, Chaplin?
Can I borrow your cane, sir?

My cane?
My lark-charmed, rook-racked, river-rounded rod?
My swish-fulfilled, fear-of-God into toothsome,
lion-limbed, lithe and wicked boys?
An odd request.

And your hat, sir?

My hat? My pudding-domed, vole-velvet bowler?
My brim-bridled, black as coal, soul-mate, balding pate-protector?
I don't see why not.

And your boots, sir.

My boots?
My cow-given, rough-scored companions of walk and toil?
My gleaming fettlers, shining out like shook foil?
Why, they're much too big for you.

The bigger the better, sir.

Glory be to God. And what, may I ask, do you intend doing
with a cane, bowler hat and a pair of oversized boots?

Pause.

Chaplin! Come back here. Chaplin! Stop acting the fool . . .
Chaplin! Chaplin!'

Cue silent-movie piano music. Roll credits.

The End

Gone but not Forgotten

Was it really that long ago?
Where the years have flown heaven only knows

We think about him often
As the nights close in and the whisky flows

O the wit of the man the yarns he could spin
About Cambridge and MI5

Undercover at Greenham Common
And lucky to get out alive

Adrift in a shark-infested
He swam and kept afloat

Until rescued by pirates
In a people-smuggling boat

Flung from the saddle at Ascot
Remounted and came in third

The night with Princess Margaret
We hung on every word

The SAS, the Hockney heist
The life and soul of the jail

Married? Only his private life
He kept beneath a veil

A God-fearing atheist
And a poet back in the day

Always a novel half finished
Thankfully remaining that way

At his best, of course, in the Red Lion
Corner table, pint of bitter in his hand

Although it might have been the Sun?
Or the Coach and Horses? Or Guinness?

How he did this-and-that and such-and-such.
Stars? He'd met them all

O the wit of the man!
The tales we would tell if only we could recall

For it is the season now of hearses and severed flowers
How each coffin looks the same

Gone, perhaps, but not forgotten
Dear old whatsisname.

Charity Shop Blues

To make it work, you must not think of the dead
nor the charity which may put you in mind of them.
Think only of the savings. Shoes by Loake
you could never afford, bespoke, slightly scuffed.
And did those feet in ancient time? Who cares?
The past removed with oxblood and a brush.

That charcoal linen suit might fit, try it on.
The jacket's fine, but one can never trust trousers.
Poor chap, he might have suffered a seizure.
Rictus, then a loosening of the bowels.
Put it back on the rail. Striped boating blazer?
No, nor tea towels with the image of Mother Teresa.

Avoid swimwear, even if it looks new. Someone
will have tried them on for size. Same applies to hats.
Bereft, a nest of Russian dolls with baby missing,
the replacement Kinder Egg no consolation.
Embroidered pillowcases, a wedding gift unopened.
The sound of sobbing would surely haunt your dreams.

And the monogrammed nightshirt? Ideal
if your initials are W.M.C. 'Bill, take a look at this,'
cried Mrs MacCaig. And the stained kimono? Oh no,
avoid it like the plague. And the mirror you are
constantly drawn to. Victorian cheval. Its retina
retains too many ghosts. Ignore it. Walk on.

Books of the deceased are acceptable. The satisfaction
to be gained from completing the final chapter
on their behalf. The previous owner gone to the grave
without knowing who dunnit. But don't be tempted
by old photograph albums. You can junk the poses
and snapped smiles, but not the imprint of their souls.

A leather briefcase, W.M.C. again. Where's Mrs Mac?
But its oppressive in here. The smell of the past,
of human musk that cannot be masked.
A cut-price mausoleum of loss and loneliness.
Time to be charitable. Hand over the bag of stuff
you want to get rid of. Feel a blessing. Walk on.

Retirement

What I love about retirement
is having so much time on my hands

What I hate about hands
is the speed at which they move around the clock

What I love about clock
is the reassurance of its surefooted rhythm

What I hate about rhythm
is the way we part company when I dance

What I love about dance
is the warm embrace of the music

What I hate about music
is its constant crying out for attention

What I love about attention
is the guardsman who stands smartly to it

What I hate about it
is IT, not Information, but Technology

What I love about technology
is how it precipitated my retirement

What I hate about retirement
is having so much time on my hands.

The Cure for Ageing

There is no cure for ageing.
Death may be incurable, but growing old is not an illness.
And some are better at it than others. The secret?
Think yourself younger than you really are:
On a crowded bus or tube, offer your seat to a young man
Help a traffic warden across a busy road
Grow cannabis in the commode
Rocking chair? Stick it up on the roof
Discreet tattoo or a gold false tooth
Design a website, invent an app
Buy your clothes from Zara and Gap
Take up Zumba, forget to nap.

Time flies they say, but it's us that fly.
Time sits on its hands as we rush by.
And life has a way of gathering speed,
So seize the day, we're a special breed.
For in the stifled yawn of a brain
The slip of a cell
The dim of an eye
The fluff of a heartbeat
You are old. Welcome to the fold.

PS if anybody says 'Well, what do you expect at your age?' Hit them.

The Old Jokes

The old jokes are the best.
The ones about demented grandads
And stairlifts. Incontinence pads
The whiff of the care home
The belch of a colostomy bag
Zimmers, commodes and the rest

The mosquito whine of a deaf aid
The grimace in a glass by the bed
The dribbly and the wrinkly
The twirly, the cauliflower head.

Ah, the old jokes are the best jokes.
For young comedians, an easy laugh.
But now I'm one of the old folks
It's not funny any more, so fuck off.

The Living Proof

Speaking as somebody who knows a thing or two
about having been your age, let me say this:
You have reached a watershed, celebrate the fact.
(Water is good for you, and everybody loves sheds.)

You can still turn heads, but over-excitement
may be a thing of the past. Forget late-night
parties, they lost their charm ages ago.
Nights are for the young and the daft.

Yours are the days, my friend, with the promise
of many more ahead. So carpe diem,
but gently, for that way they last longer.
And don't count them, just be thankful.

In fact, days can be surprisingly perfect,
arriving fully formed when least expected.
A chance meeting may be involved, a compliment
out of the blue. You make somebody laugh.

The earth need not move, no call for
fanfares and fireworks. The perfect day
can be as ordinary as a stroll by the river,
as simple as the absence of bad news.

Happy to push yourself well within your limits,
take no for an answer, and suffer fools gladly.
Content at last in the knowledge
that you are the living proof of yourself.

A Waste of Time

I don't want to waste your time,
but now that you are here
we must try to think of a way.

To think of a way of not forgetting.
Not the dead necessarily, but the out-of-touch.
Friends from our youth, grown old as we have,
living in homes we shall never visit.

Sheila Cunningham is now almost forgotten.
As is Brian Quinn who joined the navy.
Tom and Nancy, are they still together?
Did it work out for Terry in Australia?

If we were to meet what would we say,
those old pals and girlfriends consigned
to the clouding cataract of memory?
(Poetry there, getting in the way.)

Better we don't. Better we stay as we are,
where, hands above its head,
the Present shuffles towards a Future,
tight-lipped and impatient.

Rather, let us peer into the Past occasionally
and wish each other well.
I am wasting your time, I can tell.

Where is My Mother?

Where is my mother in all these poems?
Good question. My father, who wouldn't
thank me for it, is outside the school railings.
And there in the backyard failing to teach me
how to box. But don't point, you'll embarrass him.

Aunts abound, gabby and gossipy, with stories
of the Blitz, mad neighbours, loss and religion.
Unsure of themselves, uniformed uncles drift in and out.
Like their fathers, buttoned-up and elusive. Grandads,
what accents did you speak with? Could you dance?

My grandmothers remain seated, amazed at their own
wit and wisdom, of tongues posthumously gifted.
Eyes closed, I count slowly to a hundred and listen
to my grandchildren hiding and giggling. In no hurry
to be caught. And my own children? What of them?

All there, four-square, out of harm's way
and long since outgrown my concerned musings.
And the one missing, my mother, where is she?
Memory fading, at the margin still, just out of sight,
The one I aim to please with every poem I write.

Big Hugs

Before I go, who do I give a hug to?
Family, obviously, big soppy hugs all round,
and relatives, including those I've never met.

Exes. Lovers and girlfriends, especially the ones
who'd rather I didn't. Classmates? Most.
Teachers? Some. Friends who have passed away,
and parents long gone? Big, big hugs.

Places. How do I give Liverpool a hug?
High-five a Liver Bird? Edinburgh,
each Fringe a playful tug? Hull Uni.,
a pat on the back? Deià, *un abrazo*?

Gigs and dressing rooms? Holidays
and hangovers? File them under memories.
Memories? Give them all a hug,
even the bad ones, it wasn't their fault.

Failures, embarrassments, anxiety and fear,
sickness and pain, you all are forgiven.
Come here. Time for a group hug.

When it's time to go, who do I give a hug to?
(Or should it be, *to whom do I give a hug?*)
Language, of course. A big hug for words,
which have been good company throughout.

And who gets the final hug, that fretful,
lingering embrace? Unable to let go,
clinging, clinging until, fighting for breath,
something dark closes in and hugs, hugs, hugs me to death.

So Many Poems, an Apology

Comes perhaps from standing next to Philip Larkin at a bus stop.
From waving not drowning, and seldom being too far out.
From sighting a mermaid behind the fish counter at Waitrose.
From being twenty, runningallthewordstogether
and thinking, There must be more to it than this.
From a proneness to ritual and sharpened pencils.
From succumbing to the joys of self-plagiarism.

From the need to craft a melodrama
out of the remembered tediousness of one's life.
From realising I may not, after all, be its patron saint.
From expecting to be corrected while telling the truth.
From taking the words right out of the mouths of others.
From feeling relaxed about being overtaken
and disarmingly modest when overrated.

From trying to prove that, if not for everyone,
it is for anyone. From lovin' the trance that I'm in.
From stepping out of the trance, able to say,
'Hey, look what I made, if you want it, it's yours.'
From turning a deaf ear to the cold call of the cliché,
a blind eye to the clown in the cupboard.
From falling for clouds. From finishing your sentences.

From wanting to write one that is too sad to read.
From a failure to calm the brain's jostling beehive.
From loitering, pen in hand, on the escalier.
From the stealth required to follow the mind that wanders.
From holding fast the instant before thought
becomes language. From the joy of making lists.
From being rubbish at suicide.

From wherever it comes, and for whatever reason,
I apologise for writing so many poems.

Acknowledgements

The story behind 'Late Night Nightmare' can be found in *Said and Done* (Random House, 2005). 'This is One of Those Poems' is a revision of 'This is One of Those', *Everyday Eclipses*, 2002. 'What Poverty My Muse Brings Forth' was first published in *On Shakespeare's Sonnets* (Bloomsbury, 2016). 'I Hear America Sighing' and 'One Unseasonably Sunny Day in March' first appeared in the *New Statesman*.

My thanks to my wife, Hilary McGough, to Mary Mount, my editor at Penguin, to Charles Walker at United Agents and to Adrian Mealing at UK Touring.

Roger McGough

SUMMER WITH MONIKA

Summer with Monika is an honest and touching portrait of a romance, charting the progress of a love affair from the delicious intimacy of the honeymoon, with the milk bottles turning to cheese on the doorstep, through the stage of quarrels, jealousy, recriminations and boredom, to the point where love is as nice as a cup of tea in bed.

Re-issued for its 50th anniversary, Summer with Monika is a hidden gem of British love poetry featuring beautiful illustrations from Children's Laureate Chris Riddell.

'McGough's trademarks: the craft worn as lightly as the crown, the jokes that are something more, the underlying heartache, the acute sense of the way time slips away' *Poetry Review*

He just wanted a decent book to read ...

Not too much to ask, is it? It was in 1935 when Allen Lane, Managing Director of Bodley Head Publishers, stood on a platform at Exeter railway station looking for something good to read on his journey back to London. His choice was limited to popular magazines and poor-quality paperbacks – the same choice faced every day by the vast majority of readers, few of whom could afford hardbacks. Lane's disappointment and subsequent anger at the range of books generally available led him to found a company – and change the world.

'We believed in the existence in this country of a vast reading public for intelligent books at a low price, and staked everything on it'
Sir Allen Lane, 1902–1970, founder of Penguin Books

The quality paperback had arrived – and not just in bookshops. Lane was adamant that his Penguins should appear in chain stores and tobacconists, and should cost no more than a packet of cigarettes.

Reading habits (and cigarette prices) have changed since 1935, but Penguin still believes in publishing the best books for everybody to enjoy. We still believe that good design costs no more than bad design, and we still believe that quality books published passionately and responsibly make the world a better place.

So wherever you see the little bird – whether it's on a piece of prize-winning literary fiction or a celebrity autobiography, political tour de force or historical masterpiece, a serial-killer thriller, reference book, world classic or a piece of pure escapism – you can bet that it represents the very best that the genre has to offer.

Whatever you like to read – trust Penguin.